On My Bike

From Land's End to John O' Groats

by
David Jordan

Cover photo:
Sue Anderson, Taynuilt near Oban.

ISBN 0 9527875 0 4

Published by David Jordan
82 Woodlands Road, Ansdell
Lytham St. Annes FY8 1DA.

Printed by Guardian Insurance Limited, Lytham St. Annes, Lancashire.
Typeset on Apple Macintosh using Adobe Pagemaker in New Baskerville.

Acknowledgments

I wish to thank (in no particular order):-

CTC (The Cyclists' Touring Club) who were an invaluable source of advice on routes, accommodation and other matters.

David Winckle of H.G. Leyland Cycles, St. Annes, who sold me the right machine, kept it well serviced, and patiently taught me basic cycle maintenance.

Joe Stansfield, friend and veteran racing cyclist of note, for encouragement and support.

Rick and Joyce Clough of Knott End, for generous publicity.

My wife Joan, who undertook the exacting duties of Administration Manager and Financial Controller, and who ran Base Camp in her spare time.

My son Henry, who took the photographs showing Exercises for my Training Programme.

My sister Penny Anderson, who typed the bulk of my manuscript, and supplied photographs taken at Worcester.

My niece Sue Anderson, for outstanding support, hospitality and photographs at Taynuilt and later at John O' Groats.

Dave Sherlock, Colin Wellock, Peter Horner and other ex-colleagues, at Printing & Stationery department, Guardian Insurance Limited, Lytham St. Annes, Lancashire who printed this book.

Len Halls of Guardian Insurance, who did such sterling work behind the scenes, and ALL MY SPONSORS, who put their money where their mouths were and helped a very worthy Charity-Romanian Challenge Appeal.

Finally, I want to pay tribute to the real hero of this story – my Raleigh "Impact" mountain bike which, despite its low price and modest specification, carried me safely throughout my journey. It never faltered or complained!

DAVID JORDAN
Lytham St. Annes 1996

To Frank

Who would have been so pleased for me

The Decision

I could retire there and then, they said, on my 62nd birthday, or I could soldier on till I was 65, or I could go at any time in between. It was up to me. I appreciated the absence of pressure, but I guessed that my Employers would prefer a man of my age to leave pretty quickly. I probed delicately to see if there were any special inducement to retire early – a few bob from under the counter, perhaps, strictly on the Q.T. of course? – but there was not.

No matter, they'd been good employers, perhaps the best I'd worked for in a long and somewhat chequered career. I could cash my AVC's for a tidy sum, I had one or two advantageous Share Options, and my small Company Pension would, when added to my wife's Pension and my State Pension at 65, suffice to keep us both in relative comfort.

And I was tired of course. My blue-collar job as a Stationery Storeman was physically exacting, and I'd begun to notice that by 3.00pm. I was invariably worn out. The days when I would rush to work of a morning, eager to tackle the day's work-load, were long since gone. The hell with it, I thought, I couldn't quite afford to retire at 62, but I would do so on reaching my 63rd birthday. That left me a year to go – ample time to prepare myself for life without work.

How would I fill the long day after Retirement? I knew that many men seemed to give up when they stopped work for good, sitting in a corner waiting for the undertaker to come and collect them, but I wanted to do something better than that. Something out of the ordinary perhaps, something I could look back on with a degree of pride. Maybe something physical.

It was a good time to take stock of myself.

I was not a natural athlete, but I was big and strong; I had always looked after myself and was in good condition for my age.

I was not a competitor – if the other fellow was faster, stronger, smarter than I, then good luck to him – but I liked to give a good account of myself.

I was certainly no achiever. Like many a man approaching the evening of his life I looked back with dismay on the wasted gifts, the missed opportunities. Yet there was still time to do something . . . .

I really don't know what made me decide on a cycling adventure – I had a bike and, to keep myself in trim, always cycled the few miles to work and back, leaving the car in the garage. Sometimes at weekends I would cycle a little farther, to Blackpool (six miles) or even Fleetwood (fifteen miles).

Perhaps it was my friend Joe Stansfield who supplied the final spark of inspiration. Although ten years older than myself Joe was still a serious cyclist, a dedicated Time Trialist, and thought his day ruined if circumstances prevented him doing his usual training ride of twenty or thirty miles.

Whatever the reason, the decision was eventually made – come retirement on my 63rd birthday I would commence serious training to prepare myself for a cycle ride from Land's End to John O' Groats.

The 1000-mile End to End (as enthusiasts call it) still has a certain cachet – some walk it, some jog it, some cycle it, some canoe it and I believe one or two have even water-skied it, but all are entitled, perhaps, to consider themselves part of a pretty elite group of human beings.

The Plan

At first I supposed vaguely that I would undertake the project in the English style, that is to say with no prior planning or organisation whatsoever, but as time passed and the idea began to acquire a momentum of its own, I realised that a more considered approach was essential.

On Joe Stansfield's advice I joined the CTC (Cyclists' Touring Club) and found their bi-monthly magazine a rich storehouse of knowledge.

Staffed by highly expert and experienced cyclists, CTC

offer a unique service to their members. If you want to know the best route from Hyderabad to Peshawar, or the nearest cycle repair shop to a remote village in the Scottish Highlands, you have only to send a stamped, addressed envelope to CTC and you will get a sensible, helpful, friendly response.

I wrote to apprise them of my intention and asked for advice. They sent me a choice of three alternative routes along with a list of Youth Hostels en route, together with recommended Bed and Breakfast addresses. I eventually drew up my own route, based mainly upon the CTC route but modified to allow overnight stops at my sister Penny's in Worcester, my home in St. Annes near Preston and my niece Sue's in Taynuilt, near Oban. My age and temperament ruled out camping and self catering, and I decided against Youth Hostels because I could not predict my location on given days with any degree of certainty. Instead, I opted for Bed and Breakfast stops – I would watch out for suitable places as dusk fell.

I set myself a Budget of around £750, assuming the journey might take the best part of three weeks, though I would try to do it in two. I allowed £30 a day for Bed and Breakfast, meals and incidentals and I allowed £75 for rail travel with the bike to Penzance (the nearest Rail station to Land's End) and a similar sum for the homeward rail journey from Wick (nearest Rail station to John O' Groats).

I would have to get fit, of course, and I looked forward to devising a suitable Training Programme.

Finally, I considered whether to invite Sponsors for Charity. At first I was reluctant to do so, mainly because I was not fully confident of my ability to complete the journey – I had visions of collapse at the half way mark, followed by an ignominious rail journey home and a shamefaced return of Sponsors' donations. I eventually hedged my bets, approaching potential sponsors on the understanding that moneys pledged would not be collected until successful completion of the project. No finish, no money!

I made clear that the cost of the journey would be

born by myself, so that all the money collected would go directly to the chosen Charity, namely Romanian Challenge Appeal, the organisation publicised on TV who work so hard to improve the plight of orphans in Romania.

I would have to learn simple bicycle maintenance – not something I could approach with confidence. My Mechanical IQ is probably around the minus 150 mark – I dare say I could knock a nail into a piece of wood, but only with difficulty. I can sometimes render a sophisticated item of technology or machinery inoperative, simply by looking at it, never mind touching it! I have long since come to terms with this little handicap, and I comfort myself with the knowledge that greater men than I have been similarly afflicted. President Nixon could never quite get the hang of unscrewing a fountain pen ready for use – his aides had to do it for him whenever he was about to sign a Treaty. Lloyd George had to let the maid tie his shoelaces, and he could never manage to open the dining room door at No. 10.

I decided that if I could learn to mend a puncture and/or fit a new inner tube, that would have to do. If more complicated repairs ever became necessary I would simply push the bike to the nearest cycle dealer.

I would undertake the journey in June, so as to take advantage of the (hopefully) good weather and the long hours of daylight.

The Bike

At that time I owned a Dawes Ambassador – a 25″ frame 5 gear machine with sit-up-and-beg handlebars.

More economical than car travel, and more dependable than any Bus service, it was really a commuter's bike. Over the ten or more years that I had owned it the Dawes had paid for itself several times over in taking me to and from work and doing the odd shopping run. It had also helped to keep me in reasonably good health. (A heart surgeon has said that cycling is the best preventative of heart disease – provided one maintains a steady pace without undue strain).

For reasons to be explained later, the Ambassador eventually proved unsuitable for the End to End, and I had to consider what kind of new bike I should purchase. Should I buy a pukka touring bike with dropped handlebars, or a mountain bike? I consulted cycling friends and (as so often happens when experts are involved) received conflicting advice. Some thought that mountain bikes were the finest thing since sliced bread – others wouldn't touch 'em with the proverbial barge pole. I eventually decided to compromise and look out for a *cheap* mountain bike, reasoning that if it proved unsatisfactory no great harm would have been done, but if on the other hand it suited me I could invest in a more expensive one next time around.

The day came when I saw a likely machine in the shop window of H.G. Leyland Cycles in St. Annes, and the proprietor David Winckle (always helpful in these matters) let me have a trial ride around the block on it. I liked it and took the plunge.

The bike was a Raleigh "Impact", a sturdy, budget price (£160) no frills, no nonsense affair with 15 gears. It had a 23″ frame (the largest size made in mountain bikes) and was therefore just right for me – I am rather tall, at 6′2″. The bike came complete with wide road tyres, not the knobbly off-road tyres one sees on most MTB's which would have been quite unsuitable for my purposes.

I bought a few accessories – pump, tool bag and tools, spare inner tubes, puncture outfit, front and rear lamps and a rear rack designed to accommodate panniers. Most importantly perhaps, a cyclo computer which showed current speed, average speed, distance covered, clock time etc. – altogether a very handy little gadget costing only a few pounds.

Later, I managed to acquire, for only £10, a pair of second hand panniers, and since I already owned a little nylon holdall which I had obtained free of charge during a Sales promotion I felt well equipped to carry necessary belongings on the journey.

Rather than buy expensive Ordnance Survey Maps, I made do with road maps taken from an old AA Members' Handbook, and they served very well.

I debated the pro's and con's of cycle helmets and eventually decided to invest in one. Opinions differ as to their efficacy, but my own view is that they must surely offer some protection against head injuries, and should therefore be worn. Cyclists are particularly vulnerable in traffic and can expect little consideration from motorists. Over the years I have come to the conclusion that most motorists leave home five minutes late in the morning – and spend the rest of the day trying frantically to make up those lost five minutes. And it's a rare motorist indeed who will make a potentially dangerous situation safe by the simple expedient of taking his foot off the accelerator. So I bought a Met Galaxy helmet for about £20. It fitted comfortably and I was well pleased with it.

The Training Programme

There are those who say that the best training for cycling is cycling, but every man has his own thoughts on these matters, and my own view is that a man should strive for a high level of basic, all-round fitness, as well as the specialised fitness which goes with his sport. He will be less likely to suffer sports injuries, and he will benefit from the extra confidence that general fitness brings.

So when I retired at the end of April, 1994, I devised a programme which comprised both on-bike and off-bike training. I trained five days a week, on the principle that training every day without a break can become a chore, and self-defeating. I was careful never to train to the point of exhaustion – sports coaches might not approve, but doctors would.

Off bike: I included some walking at a brisk pace; for

upper-body strength I did weight training with dumbbells.

On bike: I started modestly, with a daily ride of about five miles, increasing the distance as I became fitter. In the early days I naively imagined that I could work up to a daily average of around 100 miles or so within about ten weeks, but it soon became apparent that this was not a realistic target. With hard work and determination the older man can achieve a surprisingly high standard of fitness, but he has only to break training for a few days to lose his edge. In my case, a couple of minor illnesses occurring within a few weeks of each other sufficed to set me back to square one. It was three or four months before I could manage 50 miles a day without undue discomfort – and then new problems arose, this time mechanical rather than physical.

The Dawes began to give trouble at this point. The chain fell off with increasing frequency and eventually broke. The spindle connecting the cranks snapped, the gears began to slip, and eventually to jam. Because of the bike's age it was difficult to obtain fully compatible spares, and the day came when I had to accept that I really needed a new bike – the coming End to End would be difficult enough without the additional burden of a suspect machine.

An unavoidable delay in delivery of accessories for the new Raleigh Impact obliged me to postpone the project until June the following year.

It was a big disappointment, but I consoled myself with the thought that my chances of success would be infinitely better with an extra 8 months training and preparation under my belt. In the event, the postponement was a blessing in disguise.

I cut down my on-bike training to a token 10 miles a day (enough in a Lancashire winter!) whilst at the same time stepping up my off-bike training. I joined the Fitness Centre attached to a local hotel and made full use of the very extensive facilities – a gymnasium with all the latest exercise machines, sauna, jacuzzi and a splendid swimming pool. I added swimming to my daily regime and found it an ideal way to round off a punishing workout.

With the advent of Spring I felt that I was ready for the final phase of my preparation – a gradual but steady increase in my daily mileage to a point where, by the middle of May, I could manage 50 miles a day and still feel I had something in reserve.

I enjoyed my long forays into the Fylde and Wyre – Blackpool, Cleveleys, Fleetwood, Kirkham, Garstang, Longridge, Whalley, Clitheroe, Lancaster, the picturesque villages of Wrea Green, Treales, Salwick, Broughton, Woodplumpton. Much has been written about the joys of cycling along quiet country lanes, the fresh air and tranquillity, the escape from the non-stop roar of traffic.

It was in the tiny hamlet of Hurst Green that I mended my first puncture. I found that I had left my pump at home and was in dismay, but a young lady at the local Post Office came swiftly to my rescue. She summoned her younger brother by telephone and he seemed to arrive in no time with a pump. A bowl of water appeared and I set about my task with a show of confidence I did not feel. In the event I located not one but three punctures, and mended them all. Within the hour I was ready to set off again. The occasion marked an important milestone in the development of my self-confidence.

In the course of my roaming I discovered that pubs are the best bet for a cyclist's lunch. Pubs have changed a great deal since I was a young man – the old spit-and-sawdust look has gone for ever, nowadays pubs offer comfortable upholstery, pleasant surroundings, good hot meals pleasantly served, and clean toilets (an important consideration for a touring cyclist, though one soon becomes expert at diving behind a convenient bush). Perhaps a few landlords cling stoutly to our traditional English conviction that the customer is a damned nuisance, to be firmly put in his place at every opportunity, but they are a dying breed.

My new mountain bike was fully equal to the demands of my now gruelling routine. The 15 gears sufficed to take me up all the steepest hills without discomfort, and I soon realised that despite its low price the Raleigh Impact was, for me at any rate, a definite winner, though I never managed to raise my average speed above 10-12mph. I was, after all, preparing myself to cover long distances without undue fatigue, and speed was really a secondary consideration.

Inevitably, I begun to suffer from that perennial scourge of the touring cyclist, the dreaded Sore Bottom Syndrome, or, as it is more elegantly called, Saddle Soreness. I found it frustrating that while my overall physical fitness was improving by leaps and bounds, I was nevertheless inconvenienced by this undignified and little-publicised complaint. I obtained a 10-page leaflet on the subject from CTC and found, once again, that opinions differ as to the best methods of prevention and cure – it's really a matter of the individual experimenting to find what helps him best. In my case, the best results came from a combination of a specially padded saddle and a pair of chamois-lined cycling shorts.

The Count-Down

By the end of May I felt that I was as fit as I was going to be, and it remained only to put a few finishing touches to The Plan.

On CTC advice, I would travel from Land's End to John O' Groats, rather than the other way about, because the prevailing winds in the British Isles usually (though not always) blow from South to North.

I believe the world record for cycling the End to End is under 48 hours, but I thought it might take me three weeks. However, I felt a little guilty at leaving my wife all alone while I was away enjoying myself (!) and I resolved to aim for overnight stops en route at Tavistock, Glastonbury, Worcester, Whitchurch, Lytham St. Annes, Penrith, Dumfries, Largs, Taynuilt, Drumnadrochit, Lairg and Reay. Allowing an extra day for mechanical breakdowns or unforeseen problems,

I would try optimistically to complete the journey in a fortnight.

Burning my boats for good and all, I booked Bed and Breakfast at the CTC-recommended Manor Hotel at Sennon, near Land's End, for the night of Friday, June 2nd.

Next step was to arrange transport for myself and the bike to Penzance – an operation I approached with some nervousness. I had visions of British Rail refusing to take the bike on the same train as myself, or, worse still, delivering me to Penzance and the bike to Inverness.

I went to Preston Station and prepared to explain my problem. Like so many other things, railway stations have changed a great deal since my youth, and when I reached the Ticket Office I found I would have to state my business through a thick plate – glass screen which was evidently designed to prevent me lobbing hand grenades into the office, though I had no intention of doing so.

The young man who dealt with my enquiry wore an expression of mingled patience and exasperation showing that he had spent several years in direct contact with the general public, but he was helpful, and keyed my requirements into his computer. As it happened, the computer was sulking at the time, and clearly reluctant to carry either me or my bike anywhere, but eventually it relented. For £68 British Rail would convey us both from Preston to Penzance, changing at Snow Hill Station, Birmingham and Temple Meads, Bristol.

My older son, Henry, had already promised transport in his estate car from Lytham St. Annes to Preston Station, so it seemed that the project was coming along nicely.

The ever-helpful David Winckle fitted new tyres to the bike for me, and carried out a Final Service, with particular attention to chain, gears and brakes. Under David's watchful eye I practised removing and replacing the front and back wheels until I could do it with confidence. Nothing then remained but to wind up my training and await the day with mounting excitement.

The Send-Off

It was morning, Friday June 2nd, and I was up with the lark. I donned the same clothing for the rail journey that I intended to wear on the bike – my old work uniform. I packed my panniers and holdall with a showerproof plastic suit, an old jacket and pair of trousers for evening wear, shirt and tie, pyjamas, spare socks and change of underwear, shaving tackle and toothbrush. There was just enough room, and I thanked my lucky stars that I would be bed and breakfasting and would not need a tent and other camping gear!

Henry arrived in good time to photograph the historic moment before loading the bike into his roomy estate car. Final wifely instructions from Joan and we were off to Preston Station – the die was cast!

I am by nature a pessimist – life has taught me that optimism is dangerous, the gloomy view is usually the wise view – and as I leaned back in Henry's car I reviewed, for the umpteenth time, all the things that might go wrong on the day. Would the car break down, obliging me to make a mad dash by cycle to catch the train? Would British Rail announce that they couldn't accommodate the bike after all, notwithstanding my Cycle Reservation? Would the bike be stolen en route? Would my connecting trains at Birmingham and Bristol leave before I could transfer the bike? In the event, none of these forebodings came to pass, and the only mishap occurred when I bought tea at the Preston Station refreshment kiosk – I grasped the plastic cup a little too firmly and it imploded, jumping several inches in the air and splashing tea all over the counter. I wondered if it were a bad omen, but the lady behind the counter brushed aside my apologies with a smile as she mopped up the mess, and she replaced the tea without charge.

A moment later my younger son Richard joined us on the platform, having driven from Manchester to help send me off. It was a very pleasant surprise, and I breathed easier – perhaps the day would go well, after all.

When my train pulled in (exactly on time!) the Pakistani guard was friendly and attentive. He showed me where to stow the bike, explaining that his little compartment would be locked throughout the journey, and no one would be allowed to enter without first attracting his attention. As I secured the bike to a fixture the train began to move and the smiling guard forwarded my farewells to Henry and Richard. I was on my way!

The journey was lengthy but without incident. Connections were on time, and I had ample time to transfer the bike, and when the train finally pulled into Penzance I realised that all my fears had been groundless. British Rail, I had to acknowledge, had risen magnificently to the occasion – they had delivered both myself and the bike to our destination, safe and sound and bang on time. True, the toilet hadn't flushed and the tap had refused to deliver water but what the hell, I thought, you can't expect luxury for £68 nowadays! I was in good spirits as I began the 12-mile cycle ride to Land's End, and even a steady drizzle failed to depress me.

Dusk had fallen but I found the Manor Hotel without difficulty, and was welcomed warmly by my host, Denis Sedgwick. He took in my bedraggled appearance at a glance, and in response to my anxious query assured me that there was ample time for me to take a bath and change into dry clothes before doing full justice to what proved a memorable dinner.

Built around 1790, the Manor Hotel is a fine historic building. Like so many Cornish houses of the period it is thought to have housed members of the smuggling fraternity, and its thick stone walls could no doubt tell many a tale.

Sensing atmosphere and romance wherever I looked, I asked Mr. Sedgwick if there were a ghost at the hotel. As a matter of fact, he replied, there were two! He personally had not seen either, but others had seen a mysterious cloaked man, with an equally mysterious dog, and a young girl aged about twelve. The ghosts were not unpleasant, but the young girl was inclined to be mischievous – she was said to waken sleepers by blowing on their faces! Two visiting mediums had confirmed the existence of "presences", and they had explained that the reason Mr. Sedgwick never saw the apparitions was that they had "accepted" him, and made a conscious decision not to bother or annoy him.

The Sedgwicks were clearly well accustomed to End to Enders of all types and Mr. Sedgwick himself had made the journey, albeit by motor car. He showed me several scrapbooks filled with photographs and postcards from End to Enders who had stayed at the hotel prior to starting and I promised to send a postcard announcing (hopefully!) my own triumphant arrival at John O' Groats.

By the time I finished my evening meal the rain had stopped, and I decided to reconnoitre the Land's End starting point, about a mile away. It was a pleasant walk in the cool night air, and I enjoyed the solitude and stillness. Walking through the deserted Leisure Complex I noticed a poster inviting people like myself to sign the famous Register before setting off on the epic journey. I had a nightcap at the Land's End Hotel and retraced my steps.

As I composed myself for sleep, I reflected that I should perhaps have asked for an early morning call. I wondered if the ghostly young girl would wake me in the manner described, but she didn't.

Perhaps I, too, had been accepted!

The Journey
Day 1 – June 3rd

Land's End – Penzance – Leedstown – Redruth – Truro –
St. Austell – Liskeard – Tavistock

I awoke early and ate a huge breakfast before making my farewells to the Sedgwick family. It was raining heavily but I was in good heart as I made my way to the Land's End starting point.

I had scarcely written my name and address in the

Register when I realised that I was not the only End to Ender making a start, even at 8am that Saturday morning.

I particularly noticed a group of about eight young people, all smartly attired in new cycling strip, lifting their machines out of two Transit vans in readiness. I was quite awed by their impressive back-up facility (they even had portable telephones) and they were perhaps equally impressed by my own lack of back-up and determined self-sufficiency. They invited me to join them but I declined with thanks, not wishing to inflict my snail's pace upon serious cyclists.

Throughout this narrative I shall be using the expression "serious cyclists" and I had better explain what I mean. I define a serious cyclist as one who:

1) Rides a highly sophisticated machine costing upwards of £1,000 (or more!).

2) Carries huge panniers costing perhaps another £500.00.

3) Wears the very latest (and correspondingly expensive) cycling strip and shoes.

4) Speaks knowledgeably of and can repair and adjust gears, brakes, spokes, pedals, sprockets and etc.

5) Cruises effortlessly at 15mph or even faster – about half as fast again as myself.

'John O' Groats or bust!' I thought and I set off with a flourish, following the direction pointed by a helpful signpost. I think it said 974 miles, although the route I had chosen would actually total 1,040 miles, including, alas, the odd wrong turning.

It would be a gross understatement to say the weather was unkind on this, my first morning. It blew what seemed at times to be a Force Ten gale. The icy wind blowing down my neck never left me, in fact it was to stay with me almost until the end of my long journey. I came to call it 'The Mistral' and looked for it every morning. Sometimes it would tease me, letting me think it had gone away, only to re-appear when I turned a corner. Long before I was half way to Scotland I began to fear that damned icy wind would leave me with a permanent rheumatism in my neck.

I had made a serious mistake in my prior planning. I had fully expected to encounter non-stop wind and rain in Scotland but I had fondly imagined that my progress through the effete South would be marked by blue skies, constant bright sunshine and gentle balmy zephyrs. I had therefore commenced my journey wearing light Summer clothing, intending to change into heavy Winter wear when I called at St. Annes en route, but my expectations were 100% wrong on both counts.

The day did not improve and once I had left Penzance and Leedstown behind me I found that the hills were becoming steeper and steeper.

I was lost for what seemed a very long time in Redruth and added several miles to my journey before finding the road to Truro. No matter, I told myself, if the first day proved to be a toughie (and it did) things could only improve later.

Because of the rain and my slow progress I was obliged to abandon a planned visit to Launceston where I had hoped to see the birthplace of Bob Fitzimmons, the Cornish Tin Miner who became Britain's only undisputed Heavyweight Boxing Champion.

Fitzimmons had spindly legs and weighed only 12 stone, but he often knocked out men stones heavier than himself. It was he who perfected the famous "shift" which bears his name, followed by the ferocious left hook to the solar plexus which won him the title from 'Gentleman Jim' Corbett.

He was one of the best light heavyweights on record, although, in the opinion of some of his contemporaries, his wife was pound-for-pound an even greater fighter than he!

I stopped at a Little Chef for a meal and was pleasantly surprised to be joined by the group of cycling End to Enders I had met at The Land's End Hotel.

We commiserated about the dreadful weather – and those awful hills, not to mention the traffic. One of their party, a young girl, had been forced off her machine by an impatient motorist (chasing those lost five minutes, no doubt) but she had pluckily re-mounted and seemed none the worse for the experience.

The young people were friendly and charming, but I sensed in them a certain unease, an underlying astonishment that an old party like myself, on a very basic machine and without back-up, was somehow keeping up with a well organised team of hot-shot riders. (Matter of fact, I was rather surprised myself, not to say absolutely astounded!)

When we parted it was still raining, and as the day wore on I became wetter and wetter. By teatime I realised that I was very tired too, but I resisted the temptation to seek Bed and Breakfast before reaching Tavistock. It would be a big psychological defeat, I thought, to stop short of my planned stopping place on the very first day of the journey. I struggled on doggedly and reached Tavistock at 7.00pm-ish, managing to get a room at the first place I tried.

Unpacking, I found that much of my spare clothing was wet. It was my own fault – I had foolishly omitted to pack my kit into plastic bags.

Fortunately, my landlady switched on a convector heater so that I could hang my clothing to dry in strategic places around my small but very pleasant room.

After a hot shower and change into now dry clothes, I took a stroll around Tavistock's pleasant town centre before relaxing with a drink in the lounge of a comfortable hotel. It had certainly been a swine of a day, I thought, but I had come through and on this first day at least, was on schedule. Perhaps tomorrow would be better!

Distance covered: 97 miles. Average speed 9.6mph.

Day 2 – June 4th

Tavistock – Moreton Hampstead – Exeter – Wellington – Bridgwater – Glastonbury

It was again raining when I left Tavistock and the Mistral was soon in evidence, but the sun appeared after lunch, shining weakly, though I was clearly in for another tough day.

Crossing Dartmoor I was shocked by the steepness of the hills which seemed to follow each other in never ending succession. In my late forties I had been something of a fell runner (strictly a tail-ender of course – nothing fancy) but I had experienced nothing to compare with the hills I had to negotiate in Dartmoor. My 15 gears were not sufficient to let me conquer every peak – time and again I would have to dismount and push the heavily-laden bike until the going became easier.

My morale plummeted, and I soon exhausted my not-inconsiderable vocabulary of barrack-room expletives in denouncing the terrain, the weather, the route and my own crass stupidity in ever thinking up such a crazy undertaking in the first place!

Once, as I trudged wearily towards the summit of what seemed the most difficult climb to date, I became conscious of a sheep watching me curiously from the side of the narrow road. Our eyes met, and the odd thought struck me that she had a kind face – I swear that for a brief moment she looked sorry for me! Certainly she gave a sympathetic bleat as I passed, but I was in no mood for pleasantries and I told her, brusquely, to shut up.

Sheep abound on Dartmoor of course, and at one point I passed a parked juggernaut full of them, all market-bound no doubt. They were bleating loudly and I wondered if they were as thirsty as I – poor things.

As I neared Exeter one of my End to Ending friends from the previous day joined me and we chatted briefly before I waved him on. We agreed that the hills had been terrible and that neither of us was in any hurry to see Dartmoor again. My new friend was particularly indignant – he had been taught at school that Ben Nevis was in Scotland but clearly it was on Dartmoor! Myself a victim of the same cruel deception I felt bound to agree, adding that there seemed to be another Ben Nevis around every corner. Even the descents brought problems – I saw once, free-wheeling downhill, that my cyclo-computer was recording a speed of 35mph – an unprecedented speed for yours truly! I was quite frightened, realising that if I hit a pot-hole at that speed I would certainly be thrown off. My helmet might protect me from head injuries but I would surely break my neck. It was a good thing David Winckle had paid special attention to my brakes during that last, all-important Service.

Life became a little easier after Exeter and I felt better after stopping for a meal, although I was surprised to find myself much less hungry than I had expected. For several days, in fact, I was to find that although I was always thirsty, my normally huge appetite was conspicuously absent. Perhaps it was the excitement of the journey, or more likely, the effect of muscular exertion sustained over a period of several days.

As evening fell I passed within a few miles of Bridgwater, riding through the curiously named villages which had seen the fleeing remnants of the Duke of Monmouth's ragged little army after the Battle of Sedgemoor in 1685.

An irrigation ditch ran alongside the road on which I cycled and I realised that it was in just such a ditch that Monmouth himself had hidden, only to be seized and taken to London by his triumphant captors. They say that when taken before the King and Queen he fell to his knees and begged for his life (fat chance!) but he died bravely enough on the scaffold, though the executioner botched the job horribly.

It was 8pm when I reached Glastonbury and I was very tired, but I was again lucky enough to get Bed and Breakfast easily, despite the lateness of the hour.

Too tired for conversation, I went straight to bed after a hot shower and slept soundly.

Distance covered: 95 miles. Average speed 9.5mph.

Day 3 – June 5th

Glastonbury – Midsomer Norton – Radstock – Bath – Stroud –
Gloucester – Tewkesbury – Worcester

I knew that I would be hard put to it to reach my sister Penny's home in Worcester by night-fall (I estimated the distance at just over 100 miles) so I left Glastonbury early.

It was a dry and rather sunny morning, albeit a little on the cold side, and it was not until mid-morning that the Mistral put in its usual appearance. I was pleased to find that the local terrain, although hilly in parts, was not nearly so difficult as that which I had been obliged to contend with on my first two days. Motorists, however, were a problem and twice within a few minutes cars flashed by at breakneck speed, missing my right elbow by inches.

I vowed grimly that if the next car knocked me off the bike and brought my little adventure to an inglorious end, I would sue the bugger!

I stopped at an attractive little pub and sat outside in the now warm sunshine to eat my lunch.

A friendly Welshman of about my own age joined me and listened with growing interest to my story, confiding that he was looking for just such a project to mark his own imminent retirement. Eyeing his double chin and sagging waistline I tried tactfully to moderate his enthusiasm. He must get absolutely fit before tackling such a venture, I told him, and I stressed that I was finding the going pretty tough, despite my careful preparation.

Scarcely had I finished my little homily when a call from his wife obliged him to excuse himself and beat a somewhat hasty retreat – I suspect his better half had guessed his intention and shared my misgivings about his physical condition.

I had hoped to spend a little time in Bath. Always a voracious reader, I had re-discovered Jane Austen after my retirement and I would have liked to visit the rooms in Royal Crescent Street, now open to the public, where she and her family had once lodged. I also wanted to see the famous Concert Room where Anne Elliot had spent a frustrating evening as she tried to juggle Captain Wentworth and her odious cousin, but it was not to be – I found that the beautiful City has now been ruined by the non-stop thunder of bumper-to-bumper traffic and, fearful for my safety, I pressed on towards Gloucester without stopping.

Gloucester Cathedral houses the tomb of that much maligned monarch, King Edward II, hideously murdered at Berkeley Castle nearby.

Unlike his famous father, Edward was neither cruel enough or devious enough to make a great king in those barbaric times, but as a man he had much to recommend him. Homosexual he may have been, but he was no cream puff – he was big and strong, fond of jousting and the manly sports. He swung his battleaxe as bravely as anyone in the bloody shambles that was Bannockburn, and while his critics say he left the field a bit sharpish once the day was lost, the same might be said of the entire English army.

It was in a cavalry charge of a different kind (the rush hour exodus from Gloucester City centre) that I somehow managed to take a wrong turning. I found myself on the road to Evesham and it was my worst map reading error to date, adding several miles (and perhaps an hour) to my journey.

As dusk fell I began to recognise symptoms of extreme fatigue – my co-ordination was becoming awkward and clumsy, and my alertness to danger was blurring. My poor neck, weakened by that confounded icy wind, was failing to support my head properly. I had to make frequent stops to rest my head on the handlebars; I began again to entertain the fear that rheumatism might become a permanent memento of my journey. (I need not have worried – I learned later that the trouble was muscular rather than rheumatic, caused by the unnatural cycling position putting the neck under strain for very long periods).

It was dark when I saw the familiar outline of Worcester

Cathedral, wherein lie the mortal remains of King John – a much nastier piece of work than poor Edward – minus two of his teeth, which were extracted by a dentist during an 18th Century exhumation. I saw them in the local museum 50 years ago and can only comment that the royal choppers looked much the same as yours and mine.

It was at Worcester that the famous battle was fought in (I think) 1651. You can still see the Commandery, Charles II's command post, and the timbered King's House where, according to legend, Charles fled through the back door just as the Roundheads ran in at the front. The story of Charles' subsequent escape, including his undignified stay in an Oak Tree (the "Royal Oak" commemorated in so many pub signs), deserves a book in itself.

Charles is usually portrayed as a frivolous, pleasure-loving lightweight, but I have always had a soft spot for him and I will digress now to relate two stories which show him in a better light:

His Queen, Catherine of Braganza, was barren, and both King and Court were gravely concerned at the lack of an heir. Eventually, the Dirty Tricks Department of the day put forward a convenient solution – they would have the Queen poisoned so that Charles could re-marry and get an heir from his new Queen! Charles scotched the idea.

He once sought help with a less weighty problem:

Whilst taking a walk with a Bishop, he pointed to a fine house which he had admired and asked if the Bishop knew the owner. Charles explained that he was looking for a discreet little out-of-town residence where he might sometimes rest from affairs of state, and entertain Nell Gwyn and other friends. The Bishop said he quite understood – he would approach the owner of the house and apprise him of the signal honour which His Majesty wished to confer upon him.

To the Bishop's astonishment, however, the owner refused to play. He was a God-fearing man, he said, and he was not about to turn his house into a brothel, not even to please the King!

Charles took the refusal in good part, and presumably made other arrangements to accommodate Mistress Gwyn, but years afterwards he approached the Bishop again, this time to announce that he was seeking someone to fill a vacancy for an important appointment, and he asked the Bishop to let him have a short list of suitable candidates.

Charles rejected all the names put to him and then asked if Mr. So-and-So, the man who had snubbed him so long ago, were not available? Surprised, the Bishop said: 'yes', but he was a stiff-necked self righteous fellow who simply would not compromise on what he took to be matters of principle and no one could work with him.

Charles persisted – the appointment needed, he said, a man of impeccable honesty and strength of character, because efforts would undoubtedly be made to corrupt him and seduce him from the path of duty. In short, said Charles, he was looking for the kind of man who would say "no!" to the King of England!

It was after 10.00pm when I reached the area north of Worcester where my sister Penny lives – but I could not find the house! I searched in vain for half an hour but managed to telephone Penny and asked her to come and collect me from the local pub.

I was exhausted and perhaps close to collapse. Never has a hot bath and comfortable bed been more welcome!

Distance covered: 113 miles. Average speed 9.5mph.

Day 4 – June 6th

Worcester – Kidderminster – Bridgnorth – Shrewsbury – Whitchurch

A good night's sleep left me feeling much better and I managed to eat a pretty good breakfast before leaving Worcester (was my appetite returning?).

My neck still troubled me and I frequently took off my

helmet to ease the strain, but I noted with some relief that despite the long distances I was now covering I had not experienced any serious problem with saddle soreness – perhaps the combination of excitement and more serious problems had diverted my attention.

The weather was acceptable and the few hills I encountered were mainly of the descending variety, thank goodness.

Most of the day was uneventful. I decided I could not spare time to stop in Shrewsbury where I might otherwise have seen "Mahim", the family home of Wilfred Owen, the soldier poet of World War One and a greater poet, I suggest, than Rupert Brooke.

It was in Whitchurch, my scheduled stopping place for the day, that I experienced the first sour note in my attempts to secure off-the-cuff Bed and Breakfast. The lady who opened the door at the Victorian villa where I first called was not unfriendly, and readily showed me a room which was acceptable, if a little drab and somewhat chilly. I explained that I had cycled from Worcester and was rather cold and damp – would she light the gas fire for me?

The reply was short and certainly to the point – "No!".

Speechless for once, I wondered what was wrong. The lady was old and quite tiny – had the appearance of a large, helmetted and strangely dressed figure frightened her? Or had she had some unpleasant experience involving fire and a previous visitor?

Whatever the reason, I quickly accepted a suggestion that I try next door, where I met with a very different reception. Mrs. Taylor, the landlady, was well accustomed to touring cyclists and their special needs, and within a minute or two I was under a hot shower. Soon afterwards I found myself sitting comfortably in the lounge before a roaring coal fire with an enormous pot of tea in front of me.

Later, I had sufficient energy for a walk towards the town centre. I called at a pleasant, comfortably furnished pub, where my stomach condescended to accept a large bowl of soup and a plateful of cheese and biscuits, followed by a tasty trifle washed down with a glass of wine and quart of draft cider.

It had not, I told myself, been a bad day, really – and I was still on schedule.

Distance covered: 70 miles. Average speed 8.9mph.

Day 5 – June 7th

Whitchurch – Warrington – Wigan – Preston – Lytham St. Annes

The Mistral was again finding my neck with unerring accuracy, but the sky was cloudless and the morning promised well. Two young rabbits scampered across the road in front of me, only a few feet from my wheel – a good omen perhaps. Hills were few and far between and I met no serious problems though I had to make three circuits of a very large traffic island before finding the correct exit.

I saw a beautiful church adjoining the road in Ashton-in-Makerfield and wheeled my machine into the lovely churchyard, so that I could eat my sandwich lunch in the sun. I had just sat myself down on a comfortable bench when a man approached and spoke to me. He was about my own age and dressed, if possible, even more casually. His speech was rather indistinct and I noticed that he dragged one foot behind him. I wondered if he were brain-damaged, or perhaps, as we used to say in the old days "a bit slow", but his physique was strong and he had a certain air about him, so when he spoke again, I beckoned him to join me.

As so often happens when one devotes a little time and patience to such people, the experience was rewarding. He spoke interestingly and well and was not in the least "slow".

He was born in Westhoughton, he said, and I was instantly all attention. I knew of Westhoughton's connection with a terrible murder (of the judicial variety, surely the worst kind).

Around the year 1830 some local weavers became incensed by the new machinery which was destroying their livelihood, and a group of them prevailed upon a crippled twelve year old boy to stand on their shoulders and break one of the mill windows with his crutch, so that they could enter and smash the hated machines.

Later they were apprehended and taken for trial to Lancaster Assizes. It was expected that they would suffer Transportation to the Colonies (had they not committed that most heinous of all crimes, damage to property?) but the learned judge, bless him, sentenced them all to death by hanging – including the boy. A contemporary newspaper covering the public execution reported that the twelve year old cripple cried for his mother as he awaited his turn on the gallows.

My own son was only twelve when I first heard the story many years ago, and the rage and indignation which consumed me then lingers even now.

My new friend was well aware of the story – it re-surfaced every few years in Westhoughton, he assured me. It would never rest and never should. I asked him if the Establishment of the day, the local Squire, Parson, Lawyer, had made any effort to intercede for the boy but he shook his head sadly – if any such effort had been made, he knew nothing of it.

He had himself been a keen cyclist in his day, and wished me well on my venture. When he was still a young man a motor car ran him down, leaving him senseless at the scene. He learned later that on regaining consciousness he had behaved strangely, shadow boxing, until an ambulance took him to hospital where, foolishly, he had made light of his serious injuries.

When war came, he volunteered for the Forces and was somehow accepted for the Army, serving as a Driver until he could no longer hide his disabilities.

The years that followed were not kind, and eventually a massive thrombosis had left him almost immobile but he would not give in – he struggled gamely to walk around the town centre each day and watch the world go by.

I sensed that he was one of those valiant spirits who are often beaten by life, but never quite defeated, and I was sorry when the moment came to say "goodbye". He offered to show me around that beautiful little church, but he understood at once when I explained the need for haste and his handshake was firm and strong when we parted.

It was on the main road out of Ashton that I had an experience of a less agreeable kind. Seeing a public convenience within the handsome park which adjoined the road, I hurried into the Gents for a pee – and hurried out again! When my retching stomach had composed itself I ventured inside again, to make sure I had not imagined the scene within, but I had not.

I take pride in being almost unshockable, and I have never been unduly troubled by the graffiti one frequently sees in such places.

I have even found it possible to admire the succinct clarity with which some people can list their special needs and preferences. I would go so far as to say that some of their illustrated messages are not entirely without literary and artistic merit, but what I saw that day can only be described as unspeakable.

I wondered why the Local Authority had not levelled the entire structure to the ground – certainly, I would have demolished it myself and without charge, had I been a local resident.

Perhaps, I thought, it had won some prestigious award ("The Filthiest Gents in England?") and was therefore to stand in perpetuity. But in that event there would surely have been a bold sign boasting of the distinction, and no doubt a stiff admission charge, but there was neither and I went sadly on my way, the mystery unsolved.

I was still pondering the problem when the last noteworthy event of the day occurred just outside Freckleton, a few miles from my home. I was trundling merrily along, and beginning to entertain thoughts of a romantic reunion with my better half, when I suffered the first (and happily last) puncture of the expedition.

Pausing only to make a few rather robust observations, I dismounted to examine the damage, which had evidently been caused by a very long thorn which had somehow travelled from hedge to road. I was really much too tired to risk my luck with puncture repairs, and I decided to remove the wheel and fit one of my spare inner tubes. The change took me over half an hour (a serious cyclist would have done it in five minutes) but when I remounted and resumed my journey, I felt, rather smugly, that I had been equal to the occasion and could face any future emergencies with confidence.

A few minutes later I was indeed re-united with my favourite landlady!

Distance covered: 80 miles. Average speed 8.7mph.

Day 6 – June 8th

Lytham St. Annes – Lancaster – Kendal – Shap

I had taken advantage of my overnight stay at home to change into warmer clothing, and for most of the remaining journey I was to wear an old Melton donkey Jacket. It may have been a sartorial disaster (fully in keeping with my already tramp-like appearance) but it was thick and warm, and I was to become very fond of it – I swear it saved me from catching pneumonia on the End to End. (In June!)

I was on familiar ground that morning, taking the quiet, secondary roads through Wrea Green, Kirkham, Treales, Bartle, Salwick and Broughton before turning North on the A6 towards my planned stopping place for the day, Penrith.

The weather was dry and sunny, though still windy, and I made good progress, safely negotiating the usual, pell-mell scramble through Lancaster's bustling city centre.

I was glad of a short stop in Kendal, another historic

and beautiful town ruined, for me at any rate, by the non-stop heavy traffic through the narrow, winding streets. I made my way to the lovely Abbey Park Gardens where I took refuge from the noise and ate sandwiches on a convenient bench.

The A6 from Kendal proved a formidable obstacle. I knew that the area around Shap and Penrith figures prominently in winter weather forecasts, being subject at times to deep downdrifts, but I had not foreseen the steepness and frequency of the hills, which reminded me forcibly of my unhappy progress across Dartmoor. The sparsity of human habitations worried me (how would I manage if I fell off the bike in the dark and broke a leg with no one around to help?) and when I reached Shap I decided to play safe and stay there overnight.

I was, for the first time, short of my planned stopping place (Penrith) but I felt confident that I could get back on schedule the following day and, give or take a few miles, I was already half way to John O' Groats!

The first three places I tried in Shap had no vacancies and I was beginning to fret a little when my fourth attempt, at a fine 300 year-old converted farmhouse with thick stone walls, proved successful, and after a hot bath I settled down for a comfortable night's sleep.

Distance covered: 78 miles. Average speed 8.8mph.

Day 7 – June 9th

Shap – Penrith – Carlisle – Longtown – Gretna – Dumfries

Skirting Carlisle, I entered Scotland in mid-afternoon and was pleasantly surprised to find that, although the Mistral was still a nuisance, the sun was shining brightly, with not a cloud in the sky.

Stopping at Gretna Green for my afternoon tea, I read

a notice announcing that marriage ceremonies could still be performed there, with very little formality and delay. I telephoned my wife, offering to go through the ceremony again, but she thanked me politely and said "No, once was enough!"

I was in good spirits when I reached Dumfries (on schedule again!) in the early evening. A small Victorian hotel caught my eye and seeing the sign "Bed and Breakfast £12.50", I stopped at once. I followed my usual practice and paid in advance. The room was £20.00 not £12.50 – perhaps it was one of the better rooms, I thought; anyway I was too tired to argue. I booked an early call at 6am, to be followed by an early breakfast at 7am.

Later, bathed and changed, I went in the Dining Room for my evening meal and things started to go wrong. My main course was served on a cold plate (always a bad sign) and my lamb chop tasted like pork, though I was assured it was not. The chop was certainly tough and my determined efforts to cut it nearly sent it flying across the room.

When the waitress asked if everything was satisfactory I said "No" and explained. Later, when I ordered a pot of tea, I asked if it could be served strong, but I had evidently gone too far this time and the girl bridled at my outrageous request.

Tea was tea, she said, and she must serve whatever the kitchen gave her. Gently, I persisted – the strength of tea was proportional to the number of teabags used, I said. For example (warming to my theme) a pot of tea made with two teabags would be twice as strong as the same pot made with only one teabag.

The waitress listened to my lecture in silence and brought me a pot of strong tea – but forgot to bring the milk.

Ah well, win a few, lose a few!

Later, wishing to buy some picture postcards, I strolled into Dumfries town centre and walked boldly into a rather smart hotel ("single room with breakfast £75.00" – oops!). The young man at Reception was quite unfazed by my appearance – perhaps he took me for an eccentric millionaire – and readily supplied my need. He also gave me written directions to find the Robert Burns House Museum which was nearby, and always eager to visit places of interest, I made my way there.

The poet had evidently lived the last three years of his life in Dumfries. It was a modest but rather attractive little house in a quiet part of town and I sat outside for several minutes, enjoying the tranquil scene.

Later, I walked a few steps towards the churchyard where the Burns Mausoleum is located, but the gate was secured with a huge padlock and chain, evidently designed to resist the incursion of a Chieftain tank. I saw the sign "Keep Out – Dangerous Building.".

Back at the hotel another disappointment awaited me – I realised too late that I did not like my room. The bed and bedding were clean, but the room had little else to recommend it. The light switch and plastic kettle were filthy. The television was new but the remote control switch appeared to have been rescued from a Corporation tip. The wash basin was badly cracked, and underneath it I found a curious plastic bag arrangement which might have been the replacement for a waste paper bin stolen, perhaps, by a previous occupant.

The heavy wooden door squealed loud enough to waken poor Burns in his Mausoleum, and whilst the door had once housed several coat hooks, these had all been removed over the years, leaving unsightly screwholes. I saw two Notices, curled and yellow with age. One gave Fire Instructions, the other listed Rules of the House. "Visitors found in hotel rooms after 6.00pm." it said, "would be charged full rate for bed and breakfast." I was flattered but not amused by what I took to be the implied suggestion that I might smuggle women into my room.

My good humour returned before I fell asleep – it was my own fault really, I should have checked the room before paying. *Caveat emptor* as they say in Blackpool!

Distance covered: 70 miles. Average speed 9.0mph.

Above: Day 3 - **Worcester.** Showing signs of strain after cycling 300 miles in 3 days.

Below: Day 5 - **Ashton.** "The filthiest gents in England?"

Above: Day 9 - **Inverary Castle.**
Ancestral home of the Argylls.

Below: Day 10 - **Taynuilt Village** near Oban.

Above: Day 11 - **Skirting Loch Etive**

Below: Day 11 - **An interlude at Connel bridge**.

Above: Day 11 - **Spean Bridge.**
The impressive Commando Memorial

Below: Day 13 - **Strath Naver.** "The countryside reminded
me of less happy days at Catterick"

Above: Day 14 - **John O' Groats at last!
(with Sue and champagne).**

Below: Day 14 - Signing the register at the famous hotel.

Above: Day 14 - **John O' Groats.**
Chatting with serious cyclists

Below: Day 14 - **Dunnet Head.** Pause for sightseeing

Day 8 – June 10th

Dumfries – Sanquar – Kilmarnock – Crosshouse – Irvine – Largs

I awoke early and busied myself writing out the post cards which I had bought the previous evening, so it did not matter when my early call failed to materialise at 6.00am. Nor was I terribly surprised when, going downstairs at precisely 7 o'clock for my early breakfast, I found both Dining Room and Kitchen deserted.

More amused than annoyed, I was debating whether to summon assistance by banging on one of the huge saucepans laid out in the kitchen when a pleasant but rather flustered lady arrived. No one had told her about the early call, she said, nor about the 7 o'clock breakfast either. I assured her it did not matter and in any case, was not her fault. I arranged to return in twenty minutes, after loading the bike, and when I did so a good breakfast awaited me.

Bringing my pot of tea, the lady whispered that she had made it strong, but was leaving an extra teabag on the plate for me, just in case. I repressed a smile – word of the fussy, cantankerous old Sassenach had clearly reached her on the hotel grapevine.

It was cold and windy when I set off (that damned Mistral again!) but not raining. I had scarcely left Dumfries behind when I saw a signpost pointing to another Burns Museum, only a quarter of a mile off the main road. This proved to be Ellisland Farm, where the poet had spent several years with his wife, Jean Armour.

Wheeling my bike up the rough track I was at once impressed with the utter tranquillity of the place, the farm looking just as it must have done in Burns' day.

This, I felt, was the real Scotland, the silence broken only by the gentle murmur of a nearby river, and later, by a huge gander who had obviously got out of bed the wrong side that morning and was quarreling fiercely with his wife. A cat scampered towards me and rolled over on her back, eager to play, but as I bent to stroke her another cat appeared from nowhere and chased her away.

Later, after a fish and chip lunch in Mauchline, I passed yet another Burns House Museum and resolved to spend a little time inside, notwithstanding my tight schedule.

I knew very little about Burns and my feelings towards him were ambivalent. I was aware of his reputation as a hard drinking womaniser, and I had seen too much of the pain and hurt caused by such men to admire them. Yet I felt that no man who had written " My love is like a red, red rose" and "Wee sleekit, tim'rous cowerin' beastie" could have been entirely bad.

I stayed half an hour in that fascinating little house. The Curator was clearly an authority on the Great Man and his works, and answered my many questions with patience and good humour. He had, she said, refused to accept payment for his work, despite the fame he achieved in his lifetime. Jean Armour never said a word against him – she seems to have accepted that he was simply one of those men for whom one woman is not enough. With all his faults, he was certainly a kind man, and perhaps on balance a good one. He died at thirty seven, probably of rheumatic endocarditis, after treatment (frequent immersion in a tub of cold water) which was just about the worst possible prescription.

I left regretting that I could not stay all day, but feeling that I now knew Burns better, and liked him better.

After all, a man's a man for all that!

It was 10pm when I reached Largs, my scheduled stopping place, but my luck held and I was hospitably received at my first attempt to secure Bed and Breakfast, though my landlady had only just returned from a holiday cruise.

The cruise had been a disaster, and like many of the other passengers, she had been taken ill with food poisoning. The Ship's Doctor had been mysteriously replaced early in the epidemic, and the Shipping line had stoutly disclaimed responsibility.

Not without experience in such matters, I feared she

would get no satisfaction from the Tour Operators either. I suggested that her best recourse might be to make loud noises on a well-known TV programme.

Distance covered: 80 miles. Average speed 8.5mph.

Day 9 – June 11th

Largs – Wemyss Bay – Dunoon – Inverary – Lochawe – Taynuilt

It was a warm, sunny morning, and after an hour or two I began to hope that my enemy, the Mistral, had left me for good, but it was not to be, and by mid morning I was glad I had brought my old donkey jacket.

By one o'clock the wind had dropped sufficiently for me to have lunch in the grounds of a charming, olde worlde hotel overlooking a beautiful Loch. Now well into Scotland I tried to analyse what I now knew to be a growing love affair with the Country.

Some of our English Lakes and mountains were just as lovely, I thought, as what I saw that day; our food and service just as good. The difference lay in the complete tranquillity (I keep using the word!) of the scene. The passing of a motor vehicle was so rare as to be a welcome diversion, very different to the non-stop thunder of traffic south of the Border.

My route took me through Inverary and I had a good view of the immense and imposing Inverary Castle, ancestral home of the Dukes of Argyll. It was, I think, in the 1950's that the incumbent Duke sued for divorce on the grounds of his wife's adultery with several men.

The subsequent proceedings became famous, daily newspaper reports proving a constant source of mingled outrage and mirth to people like myself, who like nothing better than to learn of scandalous goings-on among The Quality.

Perhaps the choicest and most hilarious revelation in the case came when photographs disclosed in Court appeared to show the Duchess stark naked, and busily engaged in an advanced form of sexual activity with an equally naked man who, because his face was not in camera, came to be known as "The Headless Man". (Scholars of the genre have speculated endlessly as to his identity but I fear this will never be established with certainty.)

The Duchess, who was not noted for strict veracity, denied at first that she was the woman in the naughty photographs but later, under cross examination, she admitted that she was. She claimed however that The Headless Man was none other than the Duke himself.

His Grace was waiting for that one, however, and he produced in Court an Affidavit signed by his doctor, who solemnly testified that he had measured his (the Duke's) member, and in his professional opinion it was significantly smaller than that of The Headless Man!

Game and set to Argyll – but not Match. He got his divorce, but his cavalier treatment of the Duchess in the witness box angered many of his peers. It was Not the Done Thing, Old Boy, not in those pre-Women's Lib days anyway, and the unfortunate Duke was kicked out of his Clubs.

It was dark before I could contact Sue, my niece, by telephone. Sue, a professional photographer and a very resourceful young lady to boot, was awaiting my arrival at her home in Taynuilt, near Oban. I was impressed when she explained on the telephone that she had arranged a reception party for me – they were enjoying a barbecue in Sue's garden, pending my arrival. Sue had also laid on the presence of a local reporter who was poised ready to interview me!

Sensing that I was very tired (in fact, nearly all-in) Sue left her barbecue, now in full swing, and drove towards me so that she could guide me in.

I was very pleased to see her when we met on the road some half an hour later. She piled my panniers and other bits and pieces into the back of her little van – a much appreciated easing of my burden – and I settled down to follow her home, at not much better than a snail's pace.

When we reached the rough track approaching Sue's bungalow, I heard loud cheering and the unmistakable wail of bagpipes – my well-dined (and clearly well oiled) Reception Party were giving me a traditional Scottish welcome!

Tired though I was I knew that I must rise to the occasion and so, summoning the very last reserves of my remaining strength, I managed a flamboyant sprint over the last fifty yards, punching the air in a victory salute before dismounting to greet my new friends.

The warmth of my reception quite overwhelmed me, providing a huge boost to my morale at a time when nine days hard effort in the saddle had perhaps taken a greater toll than I had realised. Sue had already approached her friends on the reception committee regarding sponsorship and, although not one of them had ever clapped eyes on me before, they all gave generously. (Who says the Scots are mean? – the very idea!)

My appetite miraculously returned to normal after a hot bath and change of clothing and I demolished most of the delicious supper (surely enough for six people?) which Sue had prepared for me.

Later, after several glasses of wine (downed in double quick time) had helped me come to terms with my now near-celebrity status, I enjoyed holding court for a while among my supporters.

Sue introduced her friend, the newspaper reporter; and his paper, The Oban Star, ran a very kind article about me soon afterwards.

Sue invited me to spend the following day at Taynuilt with her and I was quick to accept, agreeing that a day's rest and recreation would do me the world of good.

Distance covered: 82 miles. Average speed 8.4mph.

Day 10 – June 12th

Taynuilt

I enjoyed a luxurious lie-in and leisurely breakfast before oiling the chain and moving parts on the bike. Then I put the bike away, determined not to touch it or even look at it until the following morning.

That done, I settled down with some complacency to the prospect of a whole day doing absolutely nothing at all, while Sue kept up a non-stop flow of food, booze and general molly-coddling – surely the ideal pick-me-up for a tired and ageing athlete feeling just a little bit past his best.

The view from every window in Sue's house was quite beautiful, and after lunch I decided to take a leisurely stroll around the quaint little village, still marvelling at the utter peace and tranquillity.

I took advantage of the opportunity to review the state of play, and I thought that in general things were going pretty well. The journey so far had been tougher than I expected, certainly, but I had stood the pace and been equal to a quite punishing schedule. The bike had behaved splendidly, and with the greater part of the journey behind me, I was now confident that I would finish in triumphant style.

They say that when you submit yourself to a severe and prolonged physical ordeal you get to know yourself better, and I was finding this to be true. On the credit side, I had learned that I had the character and the will-power to press a difficult and arduous project through to a successful conclusion. On the debit side, I could not deny that prolonged stress made me impatient and even irascible.

I have written elsewhere about my tense encounters with the motoring fraternity. In the course of my long journey I also found myself waging what I can only describe as a one-man war against British Telecoms!

From the outset I tried to telephone my wife at least once a day, and certainly every evening, to let her know where I was and to assure her that I was safe and well, and not lying hurt and bleeding somewhere, under a car or lorry. In practice, however, I found that while it was easy to find a public telephone, it was immensely difficult to get through!

Some call boxes were "engaged" and fair enough, but some would only accept BT charge cards, and since I was not prepared to pay a minimum of 50p for a 20p call, I would not, on principle, use them. (I am a Yorkshireman, albeit only by marriage).

Cash call boxes, however presented their own difficulties – I realised after a day or two that BT were using different telephone machines, each demanding different procedures. Some would only "play" if I pressed a certain button, some would only play if I did not press the button. Some would only play if I inserted money before my wife replied, some would only play if I inserted after she replied, and some machines would not accept my money at all.

Sometimes, and worst of all, a woman with a posh voice would announce that the 'numbah' I had dialled was incorrect, her tone implying that I was some kind of moronic half-wit who should not be allowed near a telephone. I came to loathe that woman – I wondered whether she ever used a call-box herself, only to hear her own voice telling her to dial the 'numbah' again!

By the time I reached John O' Groats I must have attempted something like forty calls, of which only twenty were successful – a clear and decisive points win for BT.

The sympathetic reader will be quick to point out that I was one lone man fighting a huge organisation with immense resources, and that is true.

It is also true that for longish periods I held my own, and even scored the occasional victory. I treasure the memory of one such experience when, twice in succession, I had failed to get through, the machine confiscating my 20p coin each time.

I was hopping mad, recalling much media comment about BT's Chairman, his huge salary, his enormous bonuses, his gargantuan share options, and I was damned if he was going to have my 40p as well!

I dialled 100 and told the operator icily that her machine had stolen my money and I wanted it back, all of it. With equal coolness (she was clearly no stranger to this particular game) the operator noted my name and address and promised to send me a full refund. (She did, under cover of a suitably grovelling letter signed by one of BT's Chief Apologisers).

I was still preening myself over my little triumph when I stopped at another call-box a few miles further on, and tried again. This time, however, the machine (incensed, no doubt, by the aspersion I had cast on its colleague down the road) refused to accept my money, returning the coin each time I dialled, until I gave up and accepted defeat. 'You can't win 'em all'.

My long struggle with BT was not without its lighter moments. I think it was Sir Winston Churchill who wrote that sometimes, across the fog of war, one felt obliged to salute a worthy opponent who, by some outstanding act of daring or chivalry, had compelled one's involuntary admiration.

Such a moment was to occur towards the end of my long journey. I had concluded a telephone call and was just congratulating myself on getting through at the first attempt (!) when, with a merry tinkle and a flourish, the machine gave me my money back.

I was touched by this friendly and unexpected gesture, coming as it did after so much strife and bitterness, and I had no hesitation in accepting it in the spirit offered.

Day 11 – June 13th

Taynuilt – Connel – Fort William – Fort Augustus

I was much refreshed after my day of rest and recreation, and my morale was high when I resumed the chase. Sue went before me for several miles in her little van, stopping every so often to take photographs and point out places of interest – having lived in Scotland for many years, she knows it well.

We parted at Connel Bridge, arranging to meet again at the famous John O' Groats Hotel, which I was now very confident of reaching on June 16th, and where Sue planned to call on her way to a Trade Show in the Orkneys.

The day went well, the Highlands at their best in the warm, clear sunshine. A friendly well-wisher told me of a useful short cut, taking several miles off my journey on the road to Appin.

Skirting Loch Crevan and Loch Linnhe I broke my journey at Fort William to eat and draw some cash from a Bank, before pressing on to Spean Bridge.

A mile or so beyond the Bridge I paused to admire the hugely impressive Commando Memorial. I had already been struck by the excellent condition of Scottish War Memorials. Even the smallest villages had somehow raised sufficient funds to honour their dead in fitting style. The names of those who had fallen in World War One, 80 years before, were still crisp and clear. In Scotland, I saw, the pride and the pain are forever fresh.

I decided to stay overnight in Fort Augustus. I was not over-tired and I was ten miles short of my scheduled stopping place, but it was nearly dark and I thought it wise not to risk a night-time mishap or mechanical failure in an area where human habitation was sparse. I found Bed and Breakfast without difficulty.

My host and hostess greeted me very courteously but were clearly affected by a recent change in their circumstances. The man of the house had had little choice but to accept his employer's offer of a promotion which would, however, entail moving to another part of the country. He and his wife were desolate at the thought of leaving their lovely home which they had so lovingly built and furnished over a period of many years.

There was little I could do to comfort them beyond

observing that Home, alas, is where the money is, and they sadly agreed.

Distance covered: 81 miles. Average speed 9.1mph.

Day 12 – June 14th

Fort Augustus – Drumnadrochit – Beauly – Muir of Ord – Dingwall – Evanton – Bonar Bridge – Lairg

The morning was warm, despite the ever-present Mistral and I guessed there might be a heat-wave by afternoon. It was not long before I discarded my donkey jacket, securing it carefully over my panniers.

Entering the pretty little village of Invermoriston I made what proved to be a serious error. Spotting a Highland Cycle Trailsign pointing to Drumnadrochit, I decided to follow it, thinking it might be more interesting than the main A82 road which stretched before me.

Within a few yards the tarmacadam surface became a rough track interspersed with chippings, and a hill of terrifying gradient (the first of many such) forced me to dismount.

After a few minutes I knew in my heart that the diversion was a total disaster. It might well have suited a fit young Serious Cyclist with 24 gears and in need of a tough Sunday morning workout, but for a weary old party like myself with a long way to go, it was hell – at least as bad as anything I had experienced on Dartmoor. Pride and obstinacy prevented me at first from turning back, but after half an hour or so I had to give up the unequal struggle and laboriously re-trace my steps to the starting point.

I cursed myself for a fool – I had thrown away the advantage of an early start from Fort Augustus and was already thoroughly tired and out of sorts, with the legendary Beauly Hill still before me, not to mention that impending heat-wave.

Back on the main road again, beside Loch Ness, I soon regained my cool. I have read that some people consider Loch Ness forbidding and even eerie, but I did not find it so. It was majestic, certainly, but calm and peaceful and those ripples on the far side of the Loch came, I saw, not from Nessie but from a small dinghy.

I rested in a pleasant little park at Beauly, eating sandwiches in the warm sunshine. The much-vaunted Beauly Hill proved a less tiring obstacle than I had feared and I was soon pedalling merrily, if none too briskly, through Muir of Ord, Dingwall and Evanton, skirting Cromarty Firth, before striking north through Ardgay and Bonar Bridge.

I stopped overnight at Lairg, happy in the knowledge that I was again on schedule and, barring accidents, I had only two days to go!

Distance covered: 85 miles. Average speed 8.00mph.

Day 13 – June 15th

Lairg – Altnaharra – Syre – Bettyhill – Reay

A fine drizzle started as I left Lairg but I was not disheartened, even when the Mistral weighed in with its most violent performance to date, rousing itself to an absolute paroxysm of fury as if it realised that it had so far failed to deter me, and my long journey was now entering its final phase.

The greater part of my route to-day would be along very narrow, rather rough second-class roads with occasional stopping places. Human habitations were few and far between, and Old Soldiers will understand when I say that the countryside reminded me of less happy days at Catterick.

I stopped at the remote and isolated Crask Inn, where I had delicious coffee and buttered scones (followed by more coffee and scones)! Later, I took my time over lunch at the Altnaharra Hotel, debating whether to stay on the same road for Tongue, or take the even rougher, but shorter, Strath Naver road via Syre. On advice I took the latter road, but was dismayed to find myself cycling for several miles along a rough, chipping surface. Ever the pessimist, I assured myself there was no way I could get through the day without a puncture or two but all went well and I congratulated myself, not for the first time, on riding a machine of such proven reliability.

At Bettyhill, where I saw open sea and golden beaches for the first time since Cornwall, I stopped for refreshment at the Bettyhill Hotel, a fine old House built in 1869. Some weather-beaten men whom I took to be crofters were propping up the bar as I entered, and I got the impression they had been there all day. I was conscious of causing a minor sensation when I boldly ordered a pint of lemonade to quench my thirst, but they were friendly enough and I settled down happily to enjoy my meal.

As dusk fell I was joined briefly by a young cyclist riding a state of the art Dawes Galaxy, with huge panniers and all the trimmings. Mark was not End to Ending but was heading for John O' Groats to meet a friend and catch a ferry to the Orkneys, where they planned to attend a Festival.

It was not easy to find Bed and Breakfast accommodation in Reay, my scheduled stopping place, but I was eventually lucky enough to catch the eye of a lady who, apparently knowing everyone in the village, pointed me in the right direction.

My new host took me through his beautifully kept garden to the garage where he stowed the bike for me. He remarked that he need not lock the garage – the bike would be perfectly safe, no one would touch it. I was quick to assure him I had already learned that Scotland is inhabited exclusively by gentlemen!

Later, after emptying a pot of tea and demolishing a large plateful of sandwiches and cakes, I related some of my adventures. I commented with enthusiasm on the kindness I had encountered north of the Border – I had heard much, I said, of Highland hospitality and I had been gratified to experience it.

My host explained that the tradition was based on geographic and climatic considerations, going back many centuries.

A traveller, cold, wet, hungry and stranded in a remote area far from home, could traditionally count upon food and shelter if he knocked at the door of a crofter's house or farm even if (Glencoe notwithstanding!) he were a Campbell in MacDonald country.

Himself a widely travelled man, he had frequently visited the USA where his daughter had married and settled in a small mid-western town. I told him of my dream of cycling across the American continent, visiting the battlefields of the Civil War en-route.

I spoke warmly of the Doughboys I had seen during World War Two. Refreshingly extravert and full of themselves, they had brought confidence and optimism with them, adding a welcome dash of colour to a drab wartime Britain. Overpaid and over here they might have been, I agreed, but not really over-sexed ('quite true' says a feminine voice over my shoulder) rather it was we, the British, I suggested, who in those far-off days were over-inhibited.

Distance covered: 67 miles. Average speed 8.1mph.

Day 14 – June 16th

Reay – Thurso – John O' Groats

I was nearly there and only the cruellest ill-luck could stop me reaching my journey's end today, and probably before lunch. My already euphoric mood was raised to dizzy heights when I realised, after my first hour in the saddle, that my old enemy, The Mistral, had gone for good!

It had ignominiously fled the field, leaving me the

undisputed victor of our long battle. I had withstood its malignant fury for a fortnight; I had taken everything it could throw at me and I was still there!

The miles seemed to roll by without effort and I was not in the least tired when I pedalled happily into John O' Groats just before noon. It was the work of a moment to park the bike before bursting triumphantly (and with a slight swagger) into the famous John O' Groats Hotel.

Clearly well accustomed to excited End to Enders, the landlord greeted me very kindly, quickly producing the Register for my signature.

I telephoned my wife to confirm the safe and victorious conclusion of my Great Adventure and, almost immediately afterwards, spotted a familiar red van entering the hotel car park – Sue had arrived as planned and almost exactly on time.

A congratulatory hug and Sue took on the role of one-woman welcoming committee, producing from nowhere a large and welcome bottle of champagne to which – almost unaided – I did full and appreciative justice.

Later, whilst busily photographing me in suitably heroic poses, Sue was able to point out various places of interest in and around the little harbour.

After a good lunch at the hotel we visited the local Intourist Office where the lady in charge booked Bed and Breakfast for us at Wick, whilst establishing that British Rail would convey myself and my bike from Wick to Preston the following day, changing at Inverness and Edinburgh, and all for £70.50.

Our business concluded, Sue drove me on a sight-seeing tour of the district, culminating in afternoon tea at a little cafe in Dunnet Head where, quickly assuming my celebrity persona, I graciously acknowledged the congratulations of well-wishers at the next table.

We returned to the hotel for an evening meal of epic proportions before driving to our accommodation in Wick.

I was finding that, despite my loud complaints about

motoring and motorists, it was very pleasant, and certainly a welcome change, to be chauffeured in comfort and without any physical exertion whatsoever.

Distance covered: 37 miles. Average speed 9.5mph.

June 17th
(Homeward Bound)

Both our alarm clocks were equal to the occasion, for Sue and I were out of bed before 5.00am(!) ready to attack the Continental breakfast left by our landlady.

Sue drove me to the station in good time for my train and I noted with relief that the station was already open and ready for business, if not exactly bustling.

As we walked, bleary eyed, along the platform, the train Guard approached us, greeting me by name and producing a hand-written note telling him all about the intrepid End to Ender and his bike. Clearly, the Intourist lady had done her work well.

My bike safely stored in the Guard's van, I settled into my seat after saying good-bye to Sue. She had done a terrific job for me, both at Taynuilt and John O' Groats, and the experience had brought us very close.

The train journey was a very long one and I might normally have found it tiresome, but frankly I enjoyed sitting down and doing absolutely nothing. Even three unsuccessful attempts to telephone my wife from Inverness Station (and another two from Edinburgh) failed to ruffle my good humour.

It was only when the train had left Carlisle that matters began to go a little awry. The train slowed down and finally stopped with a weary moan. The steward announced over the Tannoy that the stoppage was due to engine failure, and we must await the arrival of engineers to repair it.

As it happened, two Senior Apologisers from British Rail were travelling on the train and they visited all compartments at regular intervals to express their regrets and update us on the state of play.

They offered to telephone my better half and explain the unavoidable delay in my return, and I learned later that they had done so – they clearly had a better understanding with BT than I!

The train eventually re-started, but could only limp along very slowly so that it was two hours late when I eventually de-trained at Preston, but I was still in philosophic mood as I retrieved the bike from the Guard's van and steeled myself for the last short leg of the journey home.

Within the hour I was indeed home at last – my long odyssey was over!

Next morning I looked drawn and underweight in the mirror, and the bathroom scales confirmed that I had lost exactly a stone, but getting back to normal was neither difficult nor unpleasant. For the best part of a week I did as little as possible, doing nothing more strenuous than lifting a mug of hot sweet tea every hour on the hour.

The missing stone quickly returned but as a precautionary measure I sounded my Doctor regarding a thorough medical. He gave the idea short shrift – I had already given myself a very thorough medical exam, he assured me, and a much more searching one than anything he could have devised. He dismissed with equally scant ceremony a timid suggestion that I might perhaps have strained something. Had I done so, he said, I would not be sitting comfortably in his Surgery, I would be lying flat on my back in a hospital bed, somewhere between Land's End and John O' Groats!

The task of calling in the sponsorship monies pledged by friends, ex colleagues and well wishers took a little time but I noted with pleasure that everyone who had promised a donation paid up. I number few millionaires among my acquaintances but the final grand total from all sources amounted to £617.20. Not a huge sum in this country perhaps, but I knew it would go a long way in Romania and I was well pleased.

I soon learned to assume a becomingly modest air when receiving the congratulations of well-wishers, and I found it interesting to compare their approach. Many gave the appearance of being quite awe-struck, as if taking me for some kind of Olympic athlete, whilst others, although too polite to say so, clearly thought I was barmy.

I was struck, however, by the number of men of my own age who shyly confided that they wanted to mark their own retirement with some similar undertaking.

It is principally for them that I have devised the End to End Training Programme which follows, though it may interest and help kindred spirits of all ages <u>and both sexes.</u>

Retirement, at whatever age, is an opportunity. Quite simply, it is an opportunity to do what you want to do. An opportunity because a priceless advantage is within your grasp – *unlimited time!*

When you are young or middle-aged, personal fulfillment must take second place to the need to earn your living and support your wife and children. Life today is tough, very tough, and whether your work is physical or cerebral the chances are that after a hard day's graft you will have barely enough energy left to meet your domestic responsibilities, let alone undertake a prolonged regime of physical exercise.

When you retire, however, you will find yourself in a very different ball game. You will have both the opportunity and the obligation to create a new life style. You can and must meet the challenge. Happily, you will (at last) have the time and the energy – always provided, of course, that you are still basically sound and healthy.

Every man will find his own road to personal fulfillment, but this part of my little book is aimed at those who, like myself, want to make a physical statement as they begin that road.

It's going to be a long, hard slog, and unless your general

health is good, this is not for you. If you have any doubts, especially about your heart and lungs, see a Doctor. Being out of condition doesn't matter – regular training will cure that – but a dodgy ticker is a very different matter, and I don't want any premature deaths on my conscience!

Take the long view and allow yourself six or twelve months, or even longer, to achieve the desired standard of physical fitness.

A word about the bike. Don't try to cycle from Land's End to John O' Groats on Grandma's old bone-shaker. You must have a modern machine with at least 15 gears. It must be of a type and size that suits you (your cycle dealer will advise), and you must feel that you can depend upon it absolutely. Buy an expensive one if money is no object, but remember that the more sophisticated the machine, the more likely it may be to break down. My own experience suggests that a down-to-earth budget-priced affair will do very well.

Learn how to mend a puncture, and better still, how to remove front and back wheel to fit a new inner tube. Never venture far from home without a pump, a puncture repair outfit, a spare inner tube or two and a few basic tools. On long journeys it is well to carry a few quid in your pocket, in case you have to stay overnight somewhere while the bike is repaired after a major breakdown or traffic accident.

Be safety-conscious. Cycling, alas, is inherently dangerous, (so is walking across the road, of course, it's a question of degree) and cyclists involved in traffic accidents are statistically much more likely to die than motorists. It is not unwise to assume that every motorist on the road may try to end your life, so check your Insurance Policy carefully – are you covered against Accidental Death or Injury "when struck by any kind of vehicle whilst a pedal cyclist on a Public Thoroughfare?"

Wear a helmet, even on short journeys, and (above all) practice manoeuvring safely in busy city centres, especially during the late afternoon rush-hour, when motorists are tired and bad tempered after a hard day's work, and eager to get home. Any indecision on your part and the buggers will cut you up rotten! They probably haven't ridden a bike themselves for years, and they've forgotten that cyclists may sometimes swerve suddenly to avoid a pothole or a pile of broken glass. So if you're in a strange town looking out for your correct lane whilst at the same time watching the traffic in front of you, behind you, and on either side of you, be extra-careful! (Eyes in the back of your head will be a distinct advantage.)

A word about *Clothing*. It is not difficult to spend the best part of £1,000 on specialist cycle clothing. If you have already been bitten by the cycling bug this might be a reasonable investment spread over several years happy enjoyment, but there is much to be said for my own clothing policy, which was simply to wear old, expendable clothing and spend (as we say in these parts) *nowt!*

You will need to set yourself a Budget, and choose a Route, taking into account your intentions regarding accommodation – Bed and Breakfast, Youth Hostels, or Camping. each has its pro's and con's.

My experience points to the advisability of allowing three weeks for the journey – a 50 miles a day limit will save you from extreme fatigue and leave ample time to enjoy people and places en route. Like the Grand National, the End to End is not just a feat of athletic endurance; it is an *experience,* so allow yourself sufficient time to savour it to the full.

What suits one will not suit another, but I will offer a few items of general advice before getting down to specifics:-
Vary your training according to the time of year – have a Winter Training Programme (October – March inclusive) with the emphasis on off - bike training. I advocate weight training, plus a little walking and swimming.

Your Summer Training Programme (April – September inclusive) will be predominantly on - bike, and as your daily mileage increases you will spend correspondingly less time on weight training, walking and swimming.

Rest is important. Try to spend two days a week doing

absolutely nothing. Not only will your body need time to re-charge its batteries, but you will need a break from what might otherwise become training drudgery. A short rest will help you to resume your routine with renewed zest and energy.

Don't train on a full stomach. Wait at least two hours after a heavy meal. Better still, perhaps, train early in the morning, when the stomach is empty. You will probably find that a mug of tea and a round or two of toast will suffice for breakfast, yet still enable you to tackle a heavy training work-load without discomfort.

A great deal is said and written about *diet* nowadays. You can scarcely read a magazine or watch TV for a few minutes without learning of some new fad or other. Your own common sense should tell you how to eat sensibly, but I venture to commend my own diet, which I have followed strictly for well over 50 years. *I eat whatever is put in front of me* and I am sure it is largely thanks to this simple diet that I have retained my strong constitution and good health for so long.

I can offer only predictable advice on smoking – *pack it in!!*

Keep a written record of your training, so that you can look back over a period to see how frequently you trained, and how far you progressed.

Finally, don't be impatient for quick results – at your age you will not achieve fitness in a few days, or even a few weeks, especially if you have neglected yourself over a long period. You can attain a very high standard of bodily performance *eventually,* but you will need to work at it harder and longer than your younger counterpart, and any prolonged break in training (because of say, illness or holidays) may take you back to square one.

Winter Programme

1)   *Walking* is a fine all-round conditioner for the older man, especially when done at a brisk pace. Begin with a gentle stroll, increasing the pace as you become fitter. Within a few weeks you should be able to manage something like Light Infantry pace – breathe deeply, swing your arms and feel your muscles working, arms, shoulders, hips and legs. You should eventually be able to maintain the pace for 20 minutes – covering perhaps a mile and a half in that time. (It is a sad commentary on our times that there are couch-potato teenagers today who are incapable of walking a mile, so don't despair if it takes some little time to progress beyond strolling pace). *Maintain Good Posture* – head up, shoulders back, hips forward!

2)   *Cycling* – again, take it steady – there is absolutely no hurry. Concentrate on acquiring a nice pedalling cadence or rhythm. If you can't keep going for half an hour at first, don't worry about it, it will come. Think Safety and hone your Road Sense. Perhaps you haven't ridden a bike since you were young – traffic conditions have changed considerably, and for the worse!

3)   *Swimming* best done at the end of the workout, it is relaxing and invigorating at the same time. Said to be one of the best forms of exercise, it forces you to breathe deeply and use all the main muscle groups. Great for heart and lungs, it goes well with weight training, perhaps because it stretches the muscles rather than contracting them. Use the back stroke sometimes, so as to work the muscles from a different angle. Easy does it, again – speed doesn't matter. Work up to 10 minutes – maybe 20 lengths in a 15 metre pool.

Warning – watch out for Ear and Eye infections!

4)   *Weight Training* (and Body Resistance Exercises) will improve your upper body strength. (Your legs, heart and lungs will get sufficient exercise from the walking, cycling and swimming).

I recommend dumbells because they are cheap, need little space, and can be used in the home. Use light to medium weights, selecting poundages which you can handle without undue strain. Gradually work up to three sets of ten repetitions per exercise. (You may have to begin with, say, one set of five – that's alright for a start).

Do each exercise methodically and rhythmically, breathing deeply. You will probably find it more comfortable to breath out when the rib-cage is being compressed, and in when it is expanding.

Take a brief rest when you feel like it – don't drive yourself to the point of exhaustion until you're fully fit, and your body can recover quickly.

There are countless variations of the ten basic exercises shown in figures 1-10, but they are outside the scope of this little book. If you would like to learn the variations (perhaps because you've become bored by a fixed routine) consult a physical culture friend or, better still, join one of the many Health Clubs now springing up all over the country. Such places usually offer a very comprehensive range of free weights (dumbells and barbells), exercise machines, swimming pool, sauna jacuzzi and so on.

Some Clubs offer preferential terms for Pensioners!

Summer Programme

After training sensibly and regularly throughout the Winter months you will have achieved a pretty high standard of what sports coaches call "core fitness", that is to say, basic, all-round fitness, as opposed to specialised fitness for a particular sport.

You have, then, only to make yourself *cycling fit* and in doing so you will be less likely, because of your existing core fitness, to suffer the strains and injuries which so often afflict the untrained man in poor condition.

Once your on-bike training work-load progresses beyond a certain level of severity (more than say, 25 miles per day) you may well find you have insufficient energy left on the day for your off-bike training. You will certainly need to scale down your off-bike training at some point, though hopefully not discard it altogether.

One solution, once you have passed the 25 mile a day mark, might be to reduce your cycle runs from five days a week to four, so that you can still devote one, or perhaps two days a week, to exclusively off-bike training.

Individuals respond to training differently, but I think the chart on the following page showing how you might progress from 5 miles a day to 50, over a period of 10 weeks, is realistic.

WEEK	Monday	Tuesday	Wednesday	Thursday	Friday	Saturday	Sunday
1	5	5		5	5	5	
2	10	10		10	10	10	
3	15	15		15	15	15	15
4	20	20		20	20	20	20
5	25	25		25	25	25	
6	30		30		30		30
7	35		35		35		35
8		40		40			40
9	45	45		45		45	
10	50	50	50	50	50		

Once you can cycle 50 miles a day on five consecutive days you're fit to tackle the End to End, so 'ON YER BIKE' and good luck!

The great thing about weight training (not to be confused with weight *lifting* which is a competitive sport) is that it needs no natural ability or special technique.
Anyone in reasonable health can do it and if you train regularly and sensibly, increasing the weights gradually, you will inevitably become stronger.

Strength, (the ability to exert force against resistance) is a powerful advantage in any sport or situation.

Interestingly, the older man can retain his strength (and to a certain extent his stamina) well into old age and certainly long after speed has, alas, become a distant memory.

Pressup (Fig 1a and 1b)
Perhaps the finest all-round conditioner known. (particularly good for arms, chest and shoulders).
Front lying, hands level with shoulders, palms flat on the floor. Straighten arms to lift body, with only palms and toes on the floor. Keep back straight. Chest must touch floor for each completed repetition after arms have been fully extended.

Lateral Raise (Fig. 2a and 2b) (for the shoulders)
Stand holding a dumbell in each hand, with arms straight at your sides. Keeping elbows locked (but not too tightly or you might strain the joints!) raise both bells sideways and upwards until they are slightly above shoulder level.

Forward Raise (Fig. 3a and 3b) (for the shoulders)
Stand holding a dumbell in each hand, with arms straight and at your sides. Keeping elbows locked (loosely), raise both bells forwards and upwards until they're at arms length overhead.

2a

2b

3a

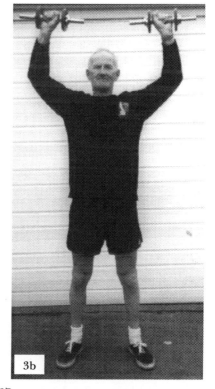

3b

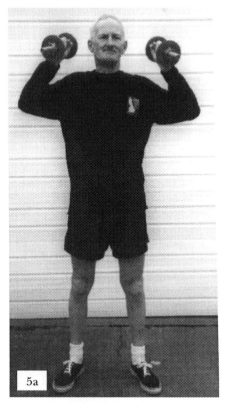

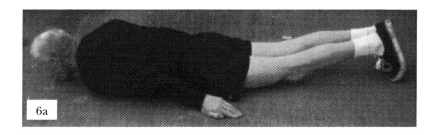

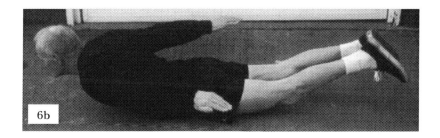

Bent Over Rowing (Fig. 4a and 4b) (for the middle back)
With a dumbell in each hand, bend over with chest parallel to the floor
and feet slightly apart. Pull bells up from the hanging position until they
touch your mid-chest, then lower and repeat.

Alternate Dumbell Press (Fig. 5a and 5b) (for the upper back and shoulders)
Stand holding dumbells at shoulder height, palms facing inwards. Press
the dumbells from the shoulders to the overhead position, lowering one
bell at the same time the other goes up.

Back Hyperextension (Fig 6a and 6b) (for the lower back)
Front lying with hands at sides, palms flat on floor. Raise head, shoulders
and legs, keeping legs straight. Both knees must clear the floor. This is a
very tough exercise, don't overdo it!

7a

7b

8a

8b

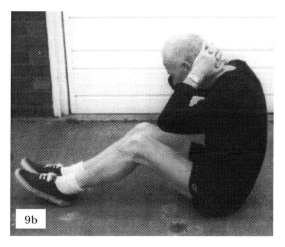

Side Bends With Stick Fig 7a and 7b
(for the 'obliques' - side-muscles).
Stand holding a broomstick across your shoulders and behind your neck. From this position, alternately bend as far as possible to left and right.

Side Twists with Stick Fig 8a and 8b (for the obliques).
Stand holding a broomstick across your shoulders and behind your neck. From this position, alternately twist your torso as far as possible to left and right. Try to keep your hips stationary throughout this exercise.

Sit ups Fig. 9a and 9b (for the upper abdominals).
Lie on your back with feet together and hands clasped loosely behind your neck. Curl your trunk upwards and forwards. Touch your knees with your forehead if you like, but it isn't essential.
Keep your knees bent throughout this exercise, to reduce the risk of back strain.

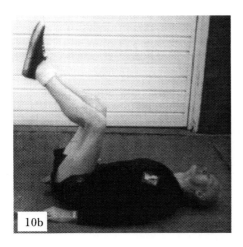

Legs Raise Fig 10a and 10b (for the lower abdominals)
Lie on your back with feet together and hands at your sides, palms
facing downwards. Slowly raise your legs to a position at least vertical,
then lower. Keep your knees slightly bent throughout - to avoid
backstrain.

Trainers have re-discovered the value of **Walking** - done at a brisk
pace it improves strength, stamina and muscle tone. It provides a
good warm-up before heavy gymnasium work, just as swimming
constitutes a useful warm **down** afterwards.
Unlike jogging, walking is both pain-free and injury - free. It can
be done throughout the year and in all weathers - so leave the car
in the garage and walk!